Dream Straw

poems by

Mariflo Stephens

Finishing Line Press
Georgetown, Kentucky

Dream Straw

ACKNOWLEDGMENTS

"Dream Straw" and "If I Can't Write" originally appeared in *Mosaic*.

Grateful acknowledgement is made to the Virginia Center for Creative Arts
for a residency where some of these poems originated or were composed.

The author would also like to thank Hollins University, Enid Shomer, and
Virginia Daugherty.

Publisher: Leah Maines
Editor: Christen Kincaid
Cover Art: Karen Levering
Author Photo: Mary Kalergis
Cover Design: Elizabeth Maines McCleavy

Printed in the USA on acid-free paper.
Order online: www.finishinglinepress.com
also available on amazon.com

Author inquiries and mail orders:
Finishing Line Press
P. O. Box 1626
Georgetown, Kentucky 40324
U. S. A.

Table of Contents

For my wonderful husband, Fred, and
my wise and beautiful daughters, Jane and Isabel

Dream Straw

I slip through the earth.
The ground suddenly straw
My feet touch my feet
Recoil howls through my chest

I'd fallen into my grave
One in a row of
Holes in a field where I walked
Falling into graves every few steps

This last grave, the straw one
Felt the worst. The others had not
Curled my toes backwards,
Thrown my hands up to my face.

On firm ground I see inside
The coffin lid sits ajar
At least, I think
Dreaming and lying, lying and dreaming,
At least keep a lid on it.

If I can't write

about my mother's last breath,
what good is this?
Of what use, this gift?

I can say she smelled sweet—
Ketosis is what it's called:
Scientifically, starvation.

I know I asked about my
father in a voice so hoarse
in the enameled hospital hall

that I almost yelled it—
        Where was he?
At home, hiding.

Phantoms, in Cars

I have seen two women
Come back
From the dead.

Both drove Volvos,
Wore sunglasses,
And long coats.

"Reetika," I said.
"You're dead."

Her look, cold, said,
And you go on.

"But your son!
You took him out.

Why? Why with
Those knives?"
The answer floats up like fireplace ash.
Because that's what
Misery loves:
Company.

Phantoms, in Cars, II

I don't believe in heaven,
but that's one way
to explain it.

When I saw you, Libby,
I was asleep;
you were so alive.

Stylish, in that green coat,
opening your car door
in front of the old dairy.

Black frames wrapped
your blue eyes
like celebrity sunglasses.

They say you did it
on a desk with
the college president.

Why? Is it true?
You reply: *If it's a lie*
It will still live longer
than I.

What If the Danger Isn't from a Stranger
for Todd

A boy's not safe
In the green house.
Hands invade and horror hovers.
A not-gentle giant presses
and a boy is injured.
Again, and again, not an accident.
And a boy's not safe
In that green house and
a boy's not safe with
his grandfather.

There was a green house and
a boy was not safe inside it.
Thirty years later that boy
still yearns to hide.
Hide from the grandfather,
hide from the hands.
Thirty years later the boy
feels small again.

Gravewalk

The ground opened up.
In a grid of graves half-hidden by straw
I fell into my own grave.
It happened in a dream
Which doesn't seem to matter.
I'd fallen into other graves
But this one
Hurt differently. The others stung but
Hadn't burned the soles of my feet.

I saw where I was in a grid of graves.
I saw who I was,
One in a long, long row.
You know. You're one in a row.
As distinctive, as unique
As straw.

Gravewalk II: Born on Labor Day, 1950

Somewhere a bird sang
The day I was born.
I doubt my mother
heard it. Deafened as
She was by those sounds:
The crank lowering
The coffin moaned.

That coffin contained
My brother, her son,
Her eldest-born child.
Even the wood of the coffin
Creaked. The preacher's back
Popped and he groaned. He's old,
She thought. He should be
In that hole in the ground.

Six weeks before my birth,
My brother died
Somewhere
In that hospital.
The doctor told my father
To wake his wife, "Tell
Her, your son is dead."
My father said no.
"Let her have one more night."
Did she ever recover? Did I?
I still want some bird to sing in September
Somewhere.

Still Bleeding

From the birth of my
Second daughter, I, a
Second daughter, answer
The phone to find
My father on the line.
"Tell your husband not to worry,"
He says. "I had three daughters
But I still had my son."

What did I say? Okay.
I've heard if you don't get
Mad, you get sad.
Elevil, Zoloft, Prozac
Xanax, Lexapro didn't work.
Taking Remeron every night,
Trying to celebrate
This life.

Tapestry, Unraveled

This hole in my life
Left by the exit of
Mother, sister, friend

Feels no better day by day.
Night is not an escape, a
Plunge into nothingness.

The hole left in my life
When my mother, my
Sister, my friend
 Left, it   this.
     Left   like
         This.   shaped
             A hole

And it's not getting filled
Any time soon. It's been
Years and I still wonder
If
    I'll
         Fall
              Out.

Orange, the New Black: Women's Prison Studies

Sheet, Blanket, Sheet
Was how we had to sleep
In the jail.

Like caulk, the cold
In that crowded jail cell
Sealed our chests.

You, a newbie, white girl
In for alcohol. Me?
Know the ropes.

Warned the warden:
"No gay for the stay, girls."
"Remember,

Sheet, blanket, sheet."
While another hooker
Winked at me

Nodding to you:
"She's been to college. Who
Says whores can't

Go to college?"
She cut you with her eyes.
"Who says? Who says?"

Dream of Youth

One night
I get it all back:
a newborn baby,
my long dead sister,

my mother too, wearing
her green dress, the paisley one.
Heaven?
We wonder together.

That night I cradled my baby
and turned in to nap beside
my sleeping sister. Heaven,
I conclude.

That night I got it all
back, my slim waist too.
"See," my mother said. "It worked
out. I even get to wear my favorite dress."

Dead, yet we still choose
what to show
the living world.

Dream of the Ages

Mother? Are you there
in this heaven where
we still pick outfits?

Then she palms that paisley collar
on that green green dress
beneath my watching eyes.

The pattern swirls and rises
off her palm; then

Spirals uncoil.
Upright now
as torsos, arms and legs.

Changing, kaleidoscope-fashion,
points and dots
become hands and feet until

On my mother's upturned hand
I watch our Scottish ancestors dance.

I, Baby Suggs
For Toni Morrison

Drained myself of words,
Run out of talk,
The kind that circles and swirls, then narrows,
Before it goes down.

I took to studying color,
Watching the rain from my bed.
Tears fall like rain too,
Water from heaven.

Rain's clear through;
It can hide but cain' lie.
I can see right through it.
Sweet William blue, dawn rose pink.

Rain's got no color, no shape,
Not like blood that spreads, reaches out,
Stain—permanent—like her ink
Telling her damn story.

Rain swells
But tears well up
Like when she said:
"I see faces in the water, my baby's faces."
My cup runnith' over.
Hers is flooded out.

Rain raises river bed;
Water seeks its own level.
Blood runs;
It doan' seek.

Excavation

To build a new school
A bulldozer moved
Raw dirt. Lifting and
Sifting everyday dirt
Every day. Until
Its claw carried a
Coffin. The driver
Leaned to his left,
Heard a crack, saw the
Dead bride fly from the
Broken coffin, smelled
The dark slurry of
What lies underneath.
First, the school had the
Dress of the dead bride
Analyzed. Fit for
A bride in 1855.
Then, she was reburied
Properly. But that
Bulldozer driver
Left excavation for
A lighter, brighter
Profession, a new job.

See that Starry Starry Night?

Dead, the tree points anyway.
Notice: it's heavenward.
Notice: The sky churns
like the sea.
Sky and sea separate except
at the horizon.
Mountains move between them.
The houses squat below.
Their lighted eyes—wise windows—see
that swirling azure sky.
See the black tree?
Broken but its
finger still points
to heaven.

River of You

I fold into his mouth.
Mine falls slack.
His hands come alive.
One cups the white cotton triangle.
The other plunges my hand under his belt.
The buckle pinches my skin, the white-blue
vein that traverses my hand like a river.
       A friend named for the state of Nevada said,
        "Some men want to don snorkel equipment when
        They go down on you."
I suppose it seems
fathoms.

Tonight we gulp air,
our bright shirts billow over the couch arms.
We slide to the floor, kick toys aside.
"Bon Voyage," I think as
his fingers sink
into the wet.
       A fathom is six feet deep
       like a grave.
       The snorkel-wearers don't see
       It's their source
       This mouth their mouth
       Is on.
Fathoms measure oceans while
I swam, unmeasured, in
a river of you.

In My Father's Coat

I walk the slow slope of his farm
Toward the woods where my sister and I, at 15,
Smoked cigarettes, kissed boyfriends,
Avoided the barns where the heavy breath
Of cows infused the purple air.

Here, now, confused by my father's coat, the black angus
Lumber downhill toward me expecting bales of hay
To slip from the coat sleeves.
I hold my empty hands up in surrender
But the cows come faster; they seem airborne.
Hundreds and hundreds of pounds hurtle for the coat.

I head for the fence. So do they. I'm almost there
When I remember that we built the fence
To pen the bull that services these night-colored beasts.
The bull! For years we ran from the bull who muddies
His caged ground stomping his huge hooves the same
Leather-gray as his heavy, swaying testicles.

Before the fence, there's a tree,
A tree I can climb. I do.
I perch for an hour in the tree.
Beneath me the cows sit like boulders.
I look over the fence to the bull pasture.
Empty? Of course. Empty for years, ever since
Men from the refrigerated truck with
"Artificial Insemination" glowingly readable to
The teenaged boys we hoped would drive by.

Those men would pull plastic gloves over their elbows,
Bring out vials of liquid, head past us for the hill,
the hill where I, now 30, strain to hear my
Step-mother shout: "It's the coat. That's what he feeds in."
I shed that coat, throw it; the cows amble away
and I climb down to see a shiny cylinder,
a shed snake skin, a snake somewhere
who, like me,
must feel re-born.

Christmas Lost

Rita Dove called to ask:
Had I found her red leather glove?
Lost at my Christmas party?

I found a green velvet button.
I made a list, then a poem.

A red leather glove,
A green velvet button,
A faithful spouse—
All lost at my Christmas party.

A tube of lipstick so pale
it couldn't be called a color.
A cell phone, a navy blue, cashmere coat,
A chenille scarf—
Ice blue, belonging

To a woman who used to be
my friend. Friends have also
Been lost
at my Christmas party.

Things left at that party:
Love, Old grudges, a new truce,
new wine, sugared peanuts:
All left
at that dad-blamed party.

Another Afternoon in May
from a painting by Barbara Grossman, 1987

Mother's in her white dress again
facing us without facing us.
She wants cards, games we let her win.
No fourth for bridge,
we could play gin.

Indigo, pumpkin, peach shadows
trace our faces, again.
It's mother's breath, reeking of gin
that lets us know an easy afternoon
is not in the cards.

Belief

The dead visit in dreams,
Advise:
"Put your carpets down."
Admonish: "See she
gets to school."

Maybe they hover
after twilight waiting
for the space between
the moon and the sun.
Maybe it's the anti-depressant.

Someone on the internet says
It's God, messages from heaven,
But I don't know.

I know only
how I dream,
what those dream visitors tell me.
Believe what you will when you
can bear to believe it.

Best Nest

In the roof of an
Unused garage, space
Cast aside.
Racoons nested there.
Unused by people but
Relished by raccoons,
That space held my poetry books.
So, raccoons nested in poetry,
sheltered there, away from
the cold and the dark.
Those animals found flowers to
feather their nests,
where they shat
on my poetry.
But I don't consider that,
deciding to focus instead on
what they found there:
their best nest.

Blind Heart

The blind piano tuner
with his mail-order
bride arrived twice a year
like royalty, his
hand resting on her
arm that she held so stiffly
I worried that it hurt her.
That he leaned on her, might
with his rotund belly,
weigh her down.
The tuning took place. Then
he played so beautifully
it broke my heart, hurting
my pride. Each time I stole
a secret happiness that his
bride's beauty never
matched his music.
That her ugliness pleased me hurt
even more than the loveliness of
her husband's songs.
What a creep I was, smiling at
the blind man's bride, her freckled arms, nob knees.

Drink Me

Softer than my own skin,
my T-shirt shows Alice with the white rabbit and
that clock. Tick. Tock.
I am old. Tick tock.
My pajama pants date back
to the Bicentennial. Yes, 1976
when I lived with a different man,
when I was a different woman,
a girl really, 26, "a woman, no child"
like what the song says.
But now my breasts have
fed two children. They look
it. Tick Tock. Then the millennium
rolled around and I turned
fifty, a round number. Just
last month a flat-chested saleswoman
found for me what she called
a T-shirt bra, which makes no
sense to me since I sleep with
Alice and that clock, tick tock.
And I plan to sleep with that funny
bunny until I sleep no more, never wake,
all for that clock's sake.

Tippy

1957-1960

Even I questioned why
I began to cry, cry, cry.
It wasn't even my dog.

So soft and perfect, that dog
looked better than when he was alive.
That's it: Sad, I wouldn't miss him.

My fear, his snarl, his bite
All gone now.
So long now,
you dog, you.

Indulgence
For My Daughters

It's true I mixed things up for you.
Not the best mother I
hid pumpkins like eggs at Halloween
decorated a tree at Easter.
But the power!
I breathed you into being;
You are answered wishes,
dreamed-up goddesses.
It took years for this question to form:
"Why did I let myself in for this?"
Some days I just can't stand it.
Then the school bus delivers
a gift at three o'clock.
But five minutes, any delay
produces the wreckage scene,
burning children trapped in the back.
The admission: "I can't keep you safe,"
hidden like a scar, unbearable.
Still we live blithely, concentrate on schools,
nutrition, information, like souls drowning on air.
Still the question comes: "Why did I let myself in for this?"
One day the answer: Surely this much love is an indulgence.

Mariflo Stephens has read or discussed her work on Oprah and the Oxygen network. Her literary work has been anthologized three times, and in 1993 she issued her own anthology, *Some Say Tomato*, which includes poems about tomatoes from Rita Dove, David Huddle, Maxine Kumin and William Stafford. Her fiction is included in *Worlds in our Words: Contemporary American Women Writers* and her essays appear in *The Barbie Chronicles: A Real Doll Turns Forty* and *Strategies for Successful Writing.*

The recipient of two grants for fiction from the Virginia Commission for the Arts, Stephens won first place in the Sherwood Anderson Short Story Contest in 2008 and won second place in 2012. She has also won prizes from the Virginia Highlands Festival and the Irene Leache Literary Contest. Her essays have aired on two public radio stations.

A former daily newspaper journalist, her work has been published in *The Washington Post, Iowa Woman, the Virginia Quarterly Review, The Walden Review, Catalyst: A Magazine for Social Change,* and *Zone 3,* among other publications. Her 1997 short story in *The Washington Review* won the Washington Review Prize for Fiction and was nominated for a Pushcart Prize. She wrote humor columns for *Iris: A Journal about Women, The Charlottesville Observer,* and *Albemarle* magazine.

In 1989 she placed second in a national short story contest sponsored by *Gamut* magazine. Stephens won The Writer's Eye contest at the University of Virginia's art museum in 1990 and judged that contest in 2003 and 2013. Stephens wrote and staged two plays for children, *Eloise's Lost Valentines* and *Sacajawea and York: Hidden Heroes of Lewis and Clark.* In 2012 her update of *The University of Virginia: A Pictorial History* was published by the University Press.

She has an M.F.A. in creative writing from the University of Virginia where she won the Thomas Griffiths Prize for the short story.